T0390124

EXTREME UNDERWATER FACTS

by Rod Barkman

BEARPORT
PUBLISHING

Minneapolis, Minnesota

Credits

Images are courtesy of Shutterstock.com. With thanks to Getty Images, Thinkstock Photo, Alamy, and iStockphoto. Recurring – Milano M, MaryDesy, Nastya Vaulina, Baskiabat. Cover – BlueRingMedia, Macrovector, Gear Digital, Bohdan Populov, KatyGr5, MrVettore, KittyVector. 4–5 – Baksiabat, NotionPic, Pogorelova Olga, Willyam Bradberry. 6–7 – David Herraez Calzada, GN.Studio, Lucia.Pinto, Maquiladora. 8–9 – Dacian Galea, Image Professionals GmbH, Morphart Creation. 10–11 – Fer Gregory, mentalmind. 12–13 – Catmando, Iconic Bestiary, Rebecca Schreiner. 14–15 – BlueRingMedia, ijimino, Invision Frame, Maquiladora, moj0j0. 16–17 – divedog, Flash Vector, Mascha Tace, NotionPic. 18–19 – alazur, Arthur Balitskii, BlueRingMedia, Oliver Denke, Lubenica. 20–21 – Craig Lambert Photography, MicroOne, nastyaartnik, Wise ant. 22–23 – Alexandre.ROSA, Kolonko, MahirAtes, Net Vector. 24–25 – Stas Moroz, wickerwood. 26–27 – Artemii Sanin, Evgeniy yes, Lillac, Wirestock. 28–29 – Julia Faranchuk, Jyggalag, Sabelskaya. 30 – Sabelskaya.

Bearport Publishing Company Product Development Team

President: Jen Jenson; Director of Product Development: Spencer Brinker; Managing Editor: Allison Juda; Associate Editor: Naomi Reich; Associate Editor: Tiana Tran; Art Director: Colin O'Dea; Designer: Kim Jones; Designer: Kayla Eggert; Product Development Assistant: Owen Hamlin

Library of Congress Cataloging-in-Publication Data is available at www.loc.gov or upon request from the publisher.

ISBN: 979-8-89232-069-6 (hardcover)
ISBN: 979-8-89232-543-1 (paperback)
ISBN: 979-8-89232-202-7 (ebook)

For more information, write to Bearport Publishing, 5357 Penn Avenue South, Minneapolis, MN 55419.

CONTENTS

INSANE, WACKY UNDERWATER WORLD

Did you know that about **71 percent** of Earth is covered in water?

There is a whole world under the waves. From huge fish to hidden **treasures**, our oceans are full of mysteries.

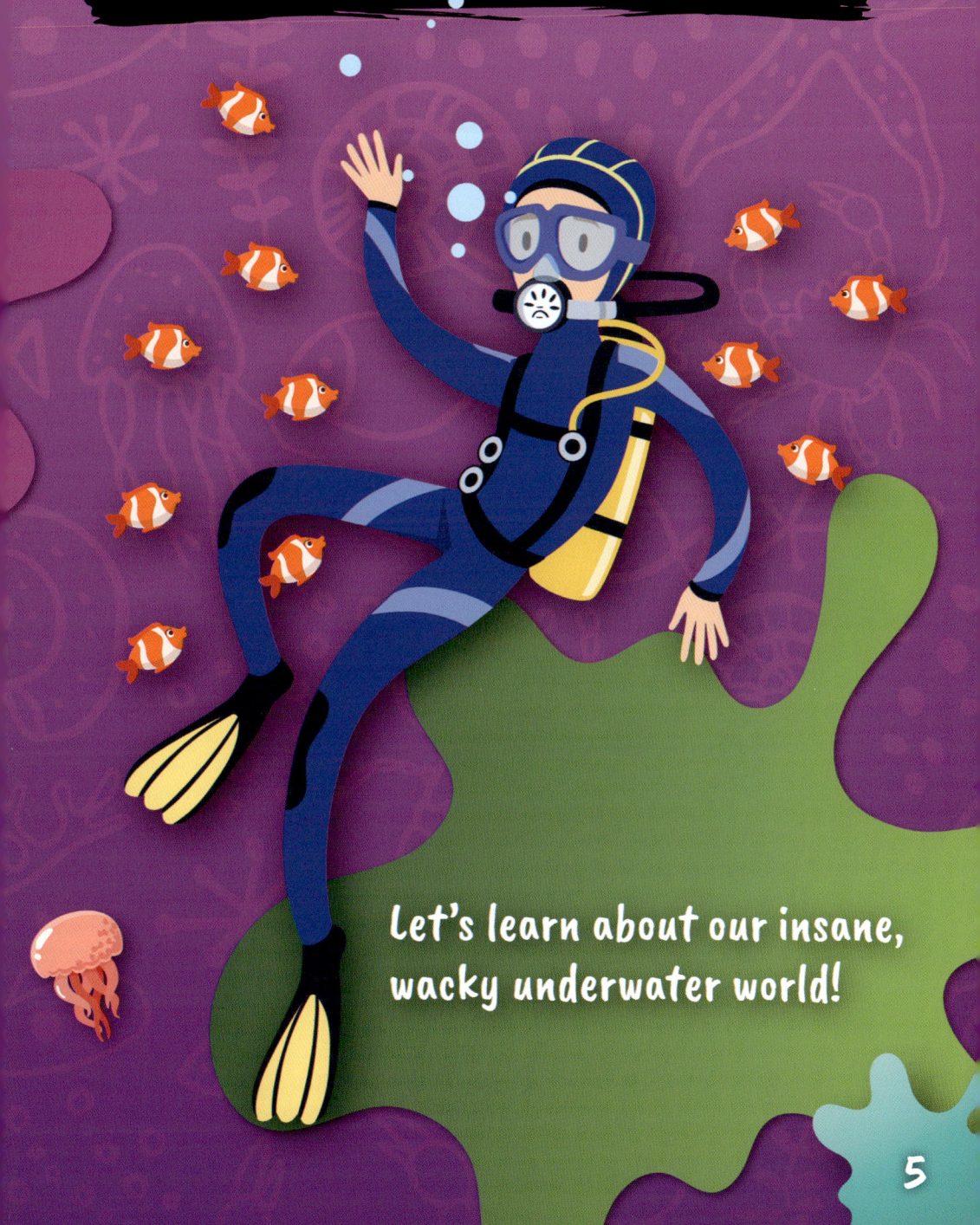

What do we actually know about the extreme waters deep down below?

Let's learn about our insane, wacky underwater world!

5

EXTREME DIVING

One way to explore the underwater world is by diving deep.

In 2014, Ahmed Gabr set a new deep dive world **record**. He went 1,090 feet (332 m) down.

EMPEROR PENGUINS CAN DIVE MORE THAN 1,600 FT. (500 M).

The name of the gear some people use to dive is called scuba.

SCUBA GEAR

What's the record for the longest scuba dive? It was 145 hours and 25 minutes!

7

EXTREME UNDERWATER INVENTIONS

All this diving had to start somewhere. But where and when did we first go down deep?

The Old Gentleman of Raahe is the oldest diving suit in the world. It was made during the early 18th century. Wooden pipes were used for breathing air.

Back in the 1600s, people used diving bells to go underwater. They trapped air in a wooden box shaped like a bell.

HOW FAR DO YOU *BELL-IEVE* IT GOES DOWN?

The Necker Nymph is the first underwater plane. It can dive 130 ft. (40 m) deep.

UNDERWATER TREASURE

Sometimes, ships sink and the treasure on board gets lost at sea.

Experts say there may be more than $60 billion in treasure at the bottom of the ocean.

WHAT KIND OF TREASURE SITS ON THE OCEAN FLOOR?

The most **valuable** underwater treasure ever found was worth $500 million. It included silver and gold coins.

FLOR DE LA MAR MEANS FLOWER OF THE SEA IN PORTUGUESE.

Some treasure hunters are looking for the sunken *Flor de la Mar* ship. People say it holds more than $3 billion worth of treasure.

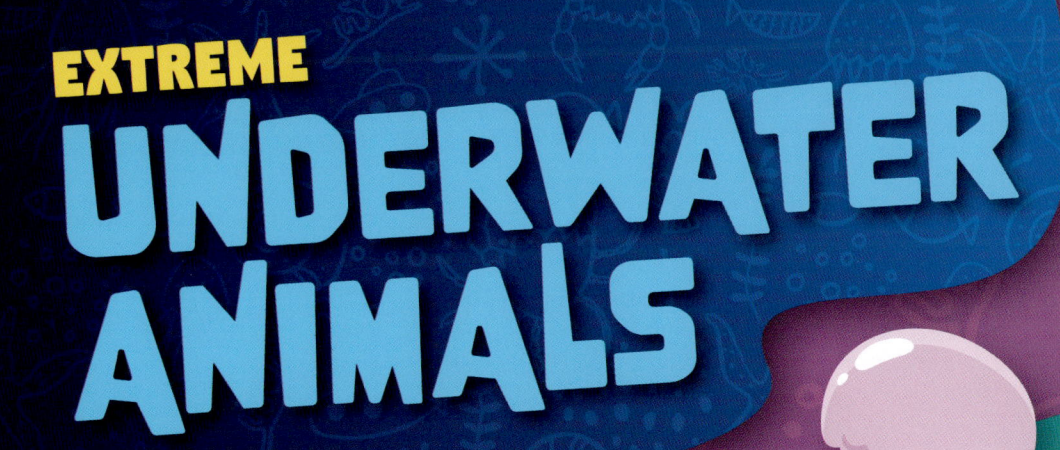

EXTREME UNDERWATER ANIMALS

The underwater world is full of some pretty extreme animals.

The immortal jellyfish is different from other animals. As an adult, this strange jelly can turn back into a baby. Then, it can grow up all over again!

Scientists thought coelacanth (SEE-luh-canth) fish were **extinct**. But in 1938, someone spotted a living one!

I'M STILL HERE!

BLUE WHALES CAN GROW MORE THAN 100 FT. (30 M) LONG.

The blue whale is the largest animal on Earth. Where is it found? Under water!

An electric eel has enough power to light six lightbulbs!

Have you heard of tongue-eating lice? They can stick to the tongue of a fish and make the real one fall off!

THIS LITTLE LOUSE BECOMES A NEW TONGUE!

14

For years, there have been stories about giant squids in the watery world down below. In 2012, a live giant squid was recorded for the first time!

Cuvier's beaked whales are deep divers. They can dive 3,300 ft. (1,000 m) down.

EXTREME PRESSURE

The deeper you go under water, the more the weight of the water presses on you. This is called pressure.

Did you know the deepest part of the ocean is 35,800 ft. (10,900 m) below sea level? The pressure there is about the same weight as if you had 48 jumbo jets on your head!

A lot of pressure changes how your body acts. It may make you feel strange.

You may get very tired or dizzy. There might also be pain in your ears, nose, or teeth.

THE MARIANA TRENCH

Let's dive to the deepest place on Earth. It is called the Mariana Trench.

THE WATER IS VERY COLD IN THE TRENCH.

It stretches along the floor for more than 1,580 miles (2,540 km). That's five times longer than the Grand Canyon!

Mount Everest is the highest point on Earth. If it ever fell into the Mariana Trench, its peak would still be 7,000 ft. (2,100 m) under the water.

CLIMBING MOUNT EVEREST IS EASIER THAN DEEP DIVING THE MARIANA TRENCH.

In the Mariana Trench, the deepest part is called Challenger Deep.

UNDERWATER SOUND

Do you think sound travels better through water or air? It moves better through water!

Sound travels even faster in the deepest parts of the ocean.

The blue whale is not only big. This animal is also one of the ocean's loudest. Its song can reach 180 decibels.

180 DECIBELS? THAT'S LOUDER THAN A JET PLANE!

In 1997, a mysterious sound was recorded underwater. It was called the Bloop. We still don't know what it was!

UNDERWATER VOLCANOES

Volcanoes are not just on land. There are more than one million underwater, too.

MOST OF EARTH'S VOLCANOES ARE HIDDEN DEEP UNDER THE OCEAN.

When underwater volcanoes **erupt,** their lava cools into volcanic glass known as obsidian.

What else can underwater lava make? It can also form islands.

THE HAWAIIAN ISLANDS WERE MADE FROM LAVA.

If a volcano at the bottom of the ocean erupts, the water it touches doesn't boil. The pressure deep underwater is too high!

UNDERWATER EXPLORATION

Most of Earth is covered in water, so there is a lot to discover under the waves.

More people have walked on the moon than have explored the floor of the Mariana Trench!

Scientists are making maps of the ocean floor . . . using sound. They use a tool called sonar to send out sound waves.

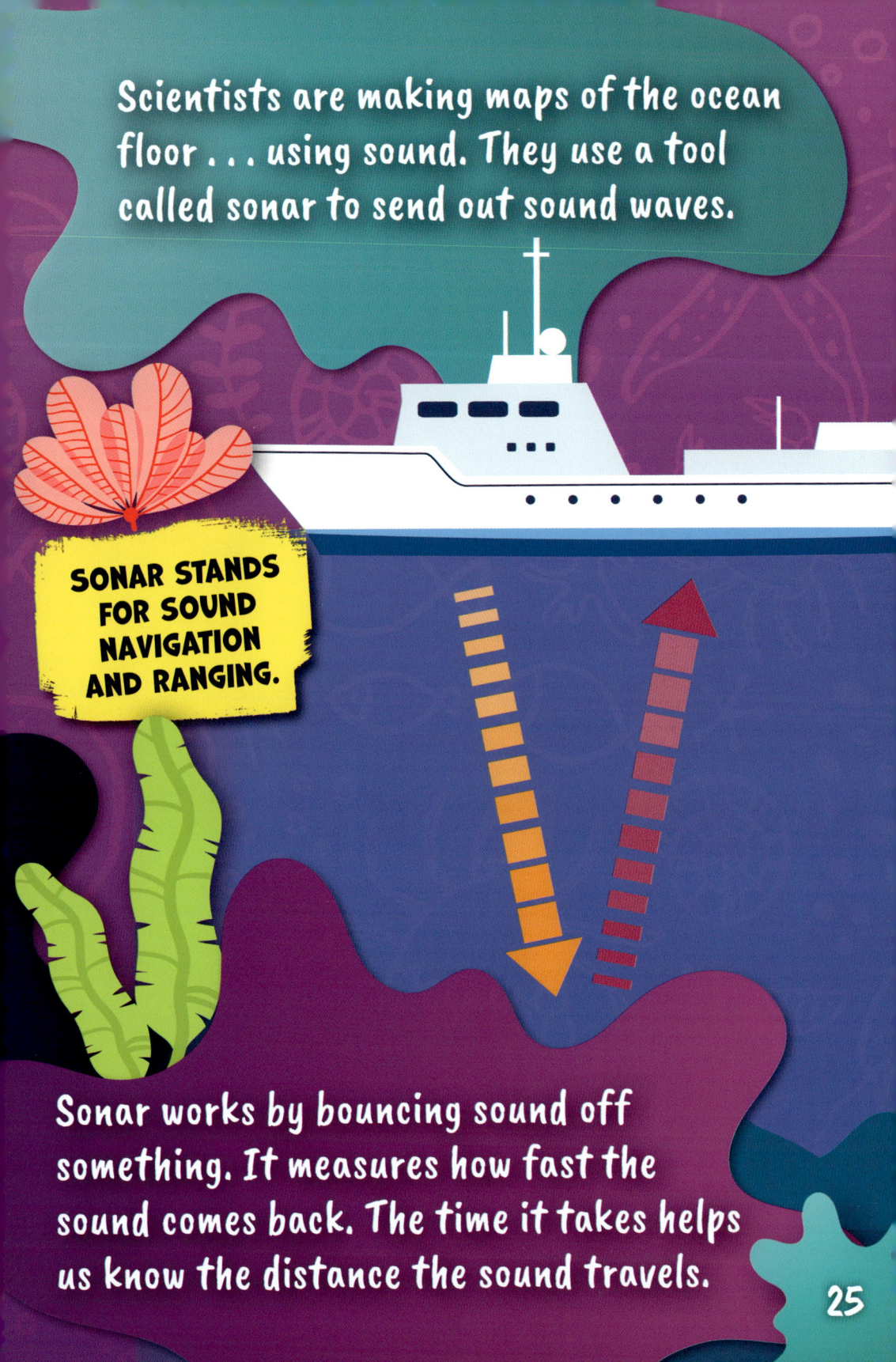

Sonar works by bouncing sound off something. It measures how fast the sound comes back. The time it takes helps us know the distance the sound travels.

THE OCEAN ZONES

The ocean has five zones. Each one is different and extreme in its own way.

As its name suggests, the sunlight zone is where the light reaches. It goes down to 660 ft. (200 m) deep.

Past the sunlight zone is the twilight zone. It goes as deep as 3,300 ft. (1,000 m) below the surface.

The twilight zone is too deep for light to reach. That's why it has no plant life.

From where the twilight zone ends until 13,100 ft. (4,000 m) is the midnight zone. It is pitch black and very cold!

THE DEEP OCEAN IS HOME TO THOUSANDS OF ANIMALS THAT GLOW IN THE DARK.

Below the midnight zone until the water is 19,700 ft. (6,000 m) deep is the abyssal zone.

What is the deepest part of the ocean? The hadal zone!

THE MARIANA TRENCH IS IN THE HADAL ZONE.

This zone is home to more than 400 known **species**. They are able to handle the extreme cold, darkness, and pressure down that deep.

UNDERWATER EXTREMES

Under the water lies a world that has yet to be discovered. It is filled with amazing creatures and lost treasures.

But since the underwater world is so big, exploring it will take a long time. That's part of what makes it so extreme!

GLOSSARY

decibels the units used to measure how loud a sound is

erupt to send out lava from a volcano

extinct when an animal has died out completely

extreme at the highest level with an element of risk

percent a part of a whole, expressed as a number out of 100

record the best achievement in a certain skill

species groups that animals and plants are divided into according to similar characteristics

treasures valuable things that are collected

valuable worth a lot of money or considered important and useful

INDEX

READ MORE

Morey, Allan. *Exploring the Deep Sea (Torque: Dangerous Journeys).* Minneapolis: Bellwether Media, 2023.

Norton, Elisabeth. *Deepest Divers (Animal Extremes).* Mendota Heights, MN: Apex, 2023.

LEARN MORE ONLINE

1. Go to **www.factsurfer.com** or scan the QR code below.
2. Enter "**Underwater Facts**" into the search box.
3. Click on the cover of this book to see a list of websites.